Ancients in Their Own

Romans

SSECONSE

ONSTREM

AMVOBISS

STRIORDI

DSVETOSE

Ancients in Their Own Words
Romans

MICHAEL KERRIGAN

mc Marshall Cavendish
Benchmark
New York

This publication represents the opinions and views of the author based on Michael Kerrigan's personal experience, knowledge, and research. The information in this book serves as a general guide only. The author and publisher have used their best efforts in preparing this book and disclaim liability rising directly and indirectly from the use and application of this book.

Other Marshall Cavendish Offices:
Marshall Cavendish International (Asia) Private Limited, 1 New Industrial Road, Singapore 536196 • Marshall Cavendish International (Thailand) Co Ltd. 253 Asoke, 12th Flr, Sukhumvit 21 Road, Klongtoey Nua, Wattana, Bangkok 10110, Thailand • Marshall Cavendish (Malaysia) Sdn Bhd, Times Subang, Lot 46, Subang Hi-Tech Industrial Park, Batu Tiga, 40000 Shah Alam, Selangor Darul Ehsan, Malaysia

Marshall Cavendish is a trademark of Times Publishing Limited

All websites were available and accurate when this book was sent to press.

Library of Congress Cataloging-in-Publication Data

Kerrigan, Michael, 1959–
Romans / by Michael Kerrigan.
p. cm. -- (Ancients in their own words)
Summary: "Offers insight into ancient times through the words of its peoples by featuring modern translations of some of the most important written records from ancient Rome, including: Aemilius's decree; the Senatus Consultum de Bacchanalibus; Marcus Caelius's Memorial; and Lutacia Lupata's Stele, with examples of Roman writing and graffiti"--Provided by publisher.
Includes bibliographical references and index.

ISBN 978-1-60870-067-7

1. Rome--Civilization--Juvenile literature. 2. Quotations, Latin--Translations into English--Juvenile literature. I. Title.

DG77.K45 2010
937--dc22

2009034428

Editorial and design by
Amber Books Ltd
Bradley's Close
74–77 White Lion Street
London N1 9PF
United Kingdom
www.amberbooks.co.uk

Project Editor: Michael Spilling
Design: Joe Conneally
Picture research: Natascha Spargo

For Marshall Cavendish Corporation:
Editor: Deborah Grahame
Publisher: Michelle Bisson
Art Director: Anahid Hamparian

PICTURE CREDITS
FRONT COVER: Main image, bust of Cicero, courtesy of Araldo de Luca/Corbis; background image, Gallo-Roman stone tablet, courtesy of The Print Collector/Alamy
BACK COVER: Funerary stela of Lutatia Lupata, courtesy of G. Nimatallah/De Agostini Picture Library

Alamy: 2 (The Print Collector), 15 (Interfoto), 43 (Peter Horree); AKG Images: 12 (Electa), 29, 31t, 32 (Gérard Degeorge), 34/35 (Peter Connolly), 56/57 (Gérard Degeorge); Art Archive: 13 (Alfredo Dagli Orti/Museo della Civilta Romana, Rome), 19 (Alfredo Dagli Orti/ Musée Archéologique, Naples), 25 (Gianni Dagli Orti/ Musée Lapidaire d'Art Paien, Arles), 38 (Alfredo Dagli Orti/ Musée Archéologique, Naples), 39 (Gianni Dagli Orti), 53 (Gianni Dagli Orti/Museo della Civilta Romana, Rome); Bridgeman Art Library: 22 (Pushkin Museum, Moscow), 52 (Bonhams, London), 54 (Giraudon) Corbis: 5 (Roger Wood), 6/7 (Nico Tondini/Robert Harding World Imagery), 16 (Francesco Venturi), 24 (Roger Wood), 41 (Mimmo Jodice), 46 (Araldo de Luca); De Agostini: 8 (G. Berengo Gardin), 9 & 17 (A. Dagli Orti), 20/21 (A. Dagli Orti), 26 (A. De Gregorio), 33 (A. Dagli Orti), 36 (Foglia), 37 (A. Dagli Orti), 45 (G. Nimatallah); Dorling Kindersley: 44 (De Agostini Picture Library), 48 & 49 (De Agostini Picture Library), 51 (Gary Ombler) Fotolia: 10 (Sam Shapiro), 31b (Markus Tappe); Getty Images: 40 (Bridgeman Art Library); iStockphoto: 23 (Zaida Pou Cufi), 42 (Luis Pedrosa), 55 (Marc Freiherr Von Martial), 58/59; Marie-Lan Nguyen: 14, 50; Photos.com: 27, 59tr; Public Domain: 18, 30; Stock.xchng: 3 & 11 (Paolo Trabalza); Hakan Svensson: 47

Printed in China
1 3 5 6 4 2

CONTENTS

INTRODUCTION

ACCORDING TO LEGEND, ROME WAS FOUNDED IN 735 BCE AND THE EVIDENCE FOUND BY ARCHAEOLOGISTS SEEMS TO AGREE WITH THIS. Remains discovered on the Palatine Hill, at the heart of the modern city of Rome, date back to around the time of the Iron Age, which began in the ninth century BCE.

The Etruscan Tarquin kings, whose heartlands lay to the north of Rome, dominated the Latin tribesmen who had come together to establish a city there. Rising in revolt, the tribesmen finally expelled the Tarquins in 509 BCE. Never again, they agreed, would they allow themselves to be tyrannized by any king. And so it was that the Roman Republic was born.

After having thrown off the Tarquin kings, the Romans themselves grew into a powerful force in central Italy. By the fourth century BCE the Etruscan threat was gone, but the growing power of Rome made its neighbors uneasy. As a result, the city was swept up in a succession of local wars. Soon Rome stood unrivaled in the Italian peninsula. But then came a conflict with the North African city of Carthage, the ancient world's most important maritime power. Between 264 and 146 BCE, Rome fought three wars against their bitter enemy. Victory over Carthage gained the Romans an empire in North Africa, Spain,

and southeastern Europe. Soon, Roman soldiers were carving out more new territories. As Roman military might expanded so did the power of the generals, and they became a threat to the ruling republicans. A series of strongmen made their bids for power and finally, in 27 BCE, Augustus became the first Roman emperor.

Imperial Power

At its height in the second century CE, the Roman Empire stretched from Scotland to Syria and from Portugal to Persia. By then there was, perhaps, no way but down. It took many lifetimes but gradually Rome's great civilization declined, suffering from internal conflict, economic problems, political rivalries, and religious turmoil. Because of its great size, the Roman Empire had vast borders and the Roman legions could barely defend them all. Barbarians took advantage of this weakness and attacked: In the fifth century CE, Barbarians repeatedly sacked Rome and finally, in 476 CE, toppled the last emperor.

◀ This carved stone head of the mythological gorgon Medusa sits inside the Severan forum at Leptis Magna, Libya. Rome had many colonies in North Africa, inherited from the Carthaginians.

GROVE OF THE GOD

THE *LEX LUCI SPOLETINA* (LAW OF THE GROVE OF SPOLETO) WAS PUT UP DURING THE FOURTH CENTURY BCE IN A GROVE THAT WAS CONSIDERED SACRED TO JUPITER.

This inscription is carved into a stone on a wooded hillside in Umbria, in central Italy, just outside the little country town of Spoleto. To this day, the forest seems a special place. The whisper of the breeze through the leaves of the holm oaks only adds to the sense of respectful calm. Eight centuries ago, Saint Francis of Assisi came here to find peace and quiet for his meditations.

▼ The Grove of Spoleto had already been sacred for centuries by the time the Romans established themselves there. This fine theater in Spoleto dates from the first century CE.

66 No one may violate this sacred grove. Do not take away or cut down anything that belongs to the wood ... Anyone breaking this law will have to offer Jupiter an ox in compensation. If someone does it deliberately he will have to pay a fine of 300 assi as well as sacrificing an ox... 99

WHAT DOES IT MEAN?

The inscription marked the boundaries of a space that was sacred to the god Jupiter. Two copies were set up on stones, one on each side of the grove, so those approaching from either direction would be warned.

▼ Quaint as it appears to us today, the severity of the Spoleto inscription would have frightened off any trespassers of twenty centuries ago.

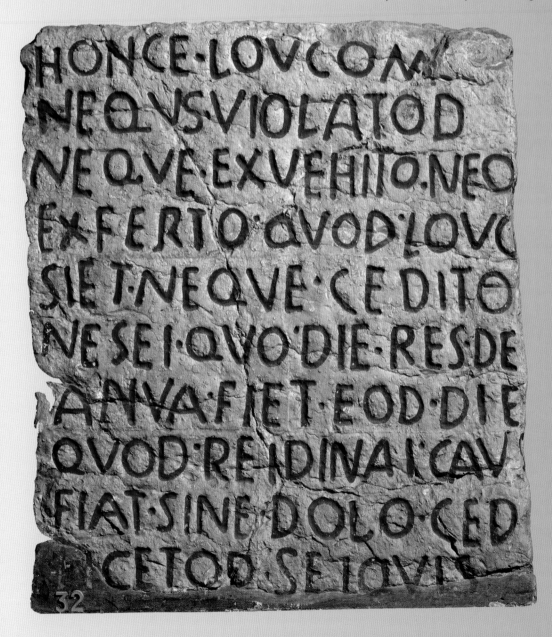

were already ancient, even in ancient times. Jupiter had roots far back in Italian antiquity, even though he is famous now as chief of the Roman deities. The holm oak had always been associated with him, and sacrifices had been offered to him in secluded groves. In Rome itself, and other big cities, worship took place in temples, while in more remote rural places older traditions lingered on.

A Common Inheritance

The Romans felt deep disdain for the Celtic peoples they conquered and for the way their priestly druids practiced their rituals in forests. In Britain, the legionaries of General Agricola systematically destroyed sacred groves. Julius Caesar, conqueror of Gaul (modern-day France), wrote contemptuously about the druids' rites, not realizing that similar practices were part of Roman tradition, too.

In fact, sacred groves have been found across the whole of Europe and much of western Asia—almost everywhere the Indo-European migrations went. (The Indo-European peoples are so-called simply because they ended up in both India and Europe.) But the Indo-Europeans originated in the steppe

An Old Tradition

But the religious associations of the grove go back much further. Archaeologists believe the Law of the Grove of Spoleto was proclaimed in 315 BCE, when the Roman Republic was still relatively young.

At that time, this part of Umbria was not yet even officially under Roman rule but was controlled by local tribes. The first reference we have to a Roman presence there dates back only to 241 BCE, when the town was known as *Spoletum*. The rituals conducted there

The Romans liked to think that they were rational, even in religion. Yet even in Imperial Rome, a priest of Jupiter had to observe odd rules. He was not allowed to ride a horse, wear rings, or have any sort of knot in his clothing or headgear. He was forbidden from touching (or even talking about) any nanny goat, and under no circumstances could he come into contact with flour mixed with yeast.

(open grassland) between the Black Sea and the Caspian Sea, in modern-day southern Russia. Some six thousand years ago, they drifted east and south into Iran and India and west into Anatolia (modern-day Turkey) and on into Europe.

These peoples went on to follow their own separate paths, developing along very different lines but, thanks to their common origins, certain likenesses remained. These include clues in the way they spoke, with unexpected similarities between what sounded like very different languages. But another common thread they all shared was the tradition of the sacred grove.

Examples have been found from India to Scandinavia and in all the countries between, including Greece and Italy. The gods worshiped by people varied from place to place, but the custom of using a grove for rituals, that was set apart from everyday life, was the same.

▼ A viaduct spans the valley of Spoleto now, but all is peaceful still. Holm oaks clothe the hillside, just as they did in Roman times.

THE FIRST ROMAN

IN THE RUINS OF POMPEII, ARCHAEOLOGISTS DISCOVERED A DEDICATION TO THE FOUNDER OF ANOTHER CITY. HIS NAME WAS ROMULUS, AND HE FOUNDED ROME AND ITS GREAT EMPIRE.

In the Chalcidicum, Pompeii's ruined record house, archaeologists unearthed an inscription commemorating the foundation of a different city altogether. According to legend, Romulus had founded Rome in 735 BCE, naming it *Roma* in his own honor. All the other cities that the Romans went on to establish in Italy and beyond were seen as later versions of Rome itself, so Romulus was revered as their founder, too.

A Tale of Twins

Romulus had originally been one of twin boys. He and his brother Remus were born early in the eighth century BCE.

◀ Rhea Silvia bore Romulus and Remus to the war god Mars. Thrown into the Tiber River with her sons, she drowned while they were saved.

THE TRANSLATION

66 Romulus, son of Mars, founded the city of Rome and reigned over it himself for some forty years. He personally slew Acro, king of the Caeninenses, at the head of his host and consecrated the regal spoils he took from him to Jupiter Feretrius. Received into the company of the gods, he is known as 'Quirinus.' 99

WHAT DOES IT MEAN?

The dedication to Romulus reminded Pompeiians that, wherever they had been born, they remained Romans, and that the empire they belonged to was first and foremost a military venture.

▶ Rome's legendary origins were part of Pompeii's heritage. As far as the Romans were concerned, in founding Rome, Romulus had founded all future Roman cities.

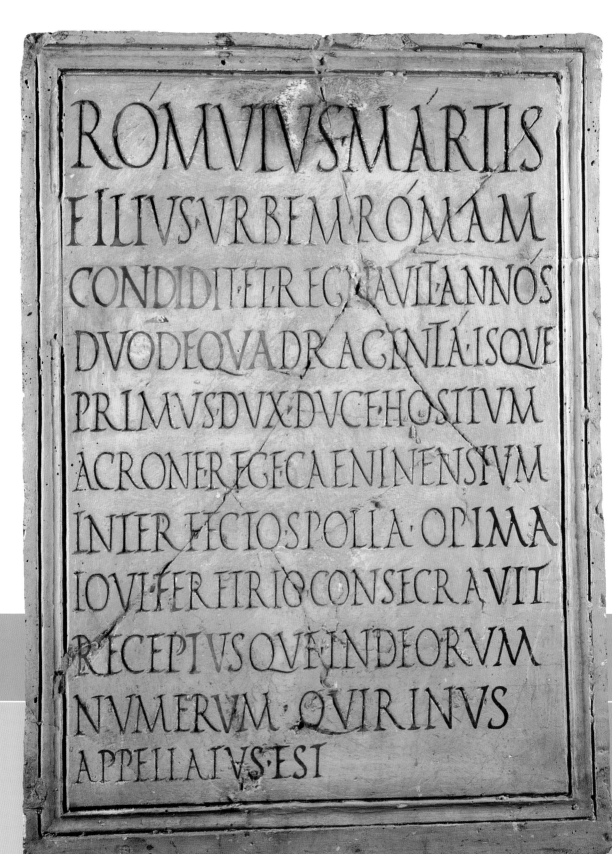

ROMVLVS MARTIS
FILIVS VRBEM ROMAM
CONDIDIT ET REGNAVIT ANNOS
DVODEQVADRAGINTA ISQVE
PRIMVS DVX DVCE HOSTIVM
ACRONE REGE CAENINENSIVM
INTERFECTO SPOLIA OPIMA
IOVI FERETRIO CONSECRAVIT
RECEPTVSQVE IN DEORVM
NVMERVM QVIRINVS
APPELLATVS EST

At that time, the greatest city in the Tiber Valley was Alba Longa, and King Numitor ruled it. The twins were born to Numitor's daughter, Rhea Silvia, but their father had been the war god, Mars. Numitor was assassinated and his throne seized by his brother, Amulius. Even though they were still just babies, Amulius feared that his nephews, Romulus and Remus, would one day be a threat, so he had them thrown into the Tiber River. But a she-wolf rescued them and reared them as her cubs.

Founded in Violence

In time the boys grew up and killed Amulius, taking revenge for the death of their grandfather, Numitor. Then the brothers started building their own city. However, they quarreled, and Romulus killed Remus. Romulus was left without a rival, the undisputed ruler of the city he now called Rome. However, he had been branded a murderer and his city's reputation had been stained. Criminals

▼ Every Roman child was told the story of Romulus and Remus. The Romans enjoyed the idea that there was something wild and violent in their origins.

and escaped slaves flocked to join him because they knew Romulus would not question their background. The followers of Romulus abducted women from nearby cities to be their wives and, over time, a thriving state emerged.

Later generations of Romans took pride in the fact that their great civilization had started out as an outlaw community. The waging of war and the taking of plunder were seen as heroic. This was why Romulus's victory over Acro, mentioned in the inscription, was so important.

Single Combat

The Romans' efficient organization, superior technology, and impressive teamwork and discipline brought them many victories in war. And, of course, they showed great courage and determination. But Romans liked to see their successes in a more romantic way, like the legendary triumphs of the heroes in ancient epic poems. Everyone knew the story of how Romulus had fought hand-to-hand with the king of the Caeninenses in single combat. And how, having defeated the king, he stripped him of his rich weaponry and armor, known as the *spolia opima* (royal spoils or plunder).

Establishing his city's first shrine, Romulus dedicated his prize to Jupiter, considered greatest of the deities. He promised that future generations of Romans would add other trophies, taken from the kings and generals of Rome's enemies, to dedicate to Jupiter.

▼ Becoming a legend in his own lifetime, Marcus Claudius Marcellus managed to do in real life what only mythical Roman warriors had done before.

DID YOU KNOW?

Only three Romans ever secured the *spolia opima*. Two of these—Romulus himself and Aulus Cornelius Cossus, who is said to have defeated Lar Tolumnius, king of the Veintes, in 428 BCE—were legends. Marcus Claudius Marcellus (c. 268–208 BCE) was the only true-life victor. He took the *spolia opima* from a Celtic chieftain in 222 BCE.

BUILDING THE REPUBLIC

APPIUS CLAUDIUS CAECUS WAS A GREAT GENERAL AND A PUBLIC SERVANT. HIS MOST PERMANENT MONUMENT IS A FAMOUS ROAD, CALLED THE APPIAN WAY.

The word "republic" comes from the Latin *Res Publicae* (the public thing). The Romans took their republic very seriously. Romulus's successors as kings of Rome had grown increasingly oppressive. Finally, in 509 BCE, the Romans rebelled, expelling Tarquinius Superbus, the last of these tyrants, who reigned from 534 to 509 BCE.

Republican Government

The new Republic was still ruled by an elite known as the paters (fathers or patricians). They elected a Senate to administer the state. Women and the working masses, many of whom were in fact slaves, had no voice. But there was no longer a single royal ruler, and the class of common people, known as the plebeians, was so large that the paters did not dare to ignore their opinion.

The Senate's first duty was safeguarding security, which could never be taken for granted. In this part of central Italy, known then as Latium, several warlike peoples, including the Samnites, the Sabines, and the Etruscans, were jostling for control of the area.

◄ In 280 BCE Appius Claudius was suddenly struck blind, earning him the agnomen (nickname) Caecus, meaning blind.

WHAT DOES IT MEAN?

Appius Claudius's stela, with its proud record of service, shows us how far personal honor and public duty went hand in hand for the Roman patrician.

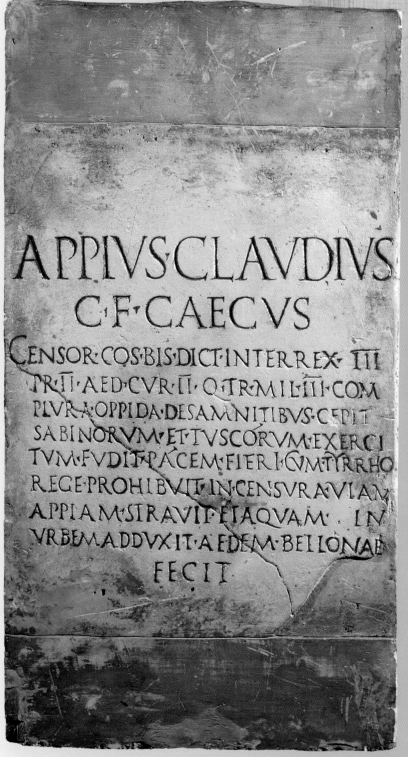

APPIVS CLAVDIVS
C·F·CAECVS
CENSOR·COS·BIS·DICT·INTERREX·III
PR·II·AED·CVR·II·Q·TR·MIL·III·COM
PLVRA·OPPIDA·DE·SAMNITIBVS·CEPIT
SABINORVM·ET·TVSCORVM·EXERCI
TVM·FVDIT·PACEM·FIERI·CVM·PYRRHO
REGE·PROHIBVIT·IN·CENSVRA·VIAM
APPIAM·STRAVIT·ET·AQVAM·IN
VRBEM·ADDVXIT·AEDEM·BELLONAE
FECIT

66 Appius Claudius Caecus, son of Caius, censor, twice consul, dictator, three times interrex, twice praetor, twice curule aedile, quaestor, three times military tribune. He took several Samnite fortresses and routed the army of the Sabines and the Etruscans; he brought about peace with King Pyrrhus; in the course of his censorship, he built the Appian Way and organized the aqueduct, which brings water to Rome. He built the Temple of Bellona. 99

◄ The savior of his state—not once but several times—Appius Claudius also did much to build its future with his extraordinarily ambitious and imaginative public works.

DID YOU KNOW?

Pyrrhus repeatedly defeated the Romans, but they had much larger forces than Pyrrhus, so their losses did less damage to their war effort than Pyrrhus's losses. These victories cost Pyrrhus too much so he had to withdraw his troops. This is known as a "Pyrrhic victory," a term that is still used to this day.

Rome was a new and minor city, but it was obviously on the rise and its neighbors saw it as a threat. Local rulers feared that Rome's republican ideals might catch on and they hoped to crush this monster before it grew.

Freedom Fighters

So began what became known as the Samnite Wars, though the Samnites fought in alliance with Rome's other enemies. The first began in 343 BCE and was won by the Romans in 341 BCE (the year before Appius Claudius was born). When he grew up, Appius Claudius became a general of courage and flair, and he commanded the Roman army in the Second Samnite

▲ The Appian Way extended all the way from Rome to Brindisi in southeastern Italy. While it helped foster trade, its primary inspiration was military.

▶ The Samnites were just one of several enemies ranked against the young Roman Republic. In the fourth century BCE Rome faced a real struggle to survive.

War of 326 to 304 BCE. The Third Samnite War broke out in 298 BCE and, once again, Appius Claudius led the Romans. He promised Bellona, goddess of war, that he would build her a beautiful new shrine if she gave him victory. When she did, in 290 BCE, he kept his word. Rome was now the dominant power in the Italian peninsula. But in 280 BCE, King Pyrrhus of Epirus in Greece (who reigned from 307 to 272 BCE) attacked across the Adriatic Sea. Appius Claudius came to the rescue, wearing down Pyrrhus's army in a long and hard campaign.

An Officer of the State

In between these heroics, Appius Claudius held nearly every one of the most important offices of state. His role as censor took its name from the fact that he oversaw the regular census of the population, but it also gave him responsibility for public morality. As a consul, one of Rome's two most senior officers of law, he was actually coruler of the Republic except when, in times of military crisis, he became sole ruler or dictator.

He was not just a dutiful public servant but also a visionary. For example, he built the Aqua Appia, the first great aqueduct, bringing fresh water from the hills outside the city. But his most famous work was a road known as the Appian Way. Appius Claudius died in 273 BCE.

FREEDOM...FOR SOME

From Cádiz, in southwestern Spain, comes a story of conquest and liberation. The inscription on this stone tablet shows the mixed blessings the Romans brought to its growing empire.

Rome very nearly did not survive to see the middle of the third century BCE. Twice, the city had come close to being crushed by Carthage, a city on the Tunisian coast founded by the Phoenicians. A Semitic trading people, the Phoenicians had originated in Lebanon, in the eastern Mediterranean.

However, Carthage, their North African colony, had soon surpassed its mother country, and its influence extended throughout the Mediterranean. Carthage had viewed the rise of Rome with deep suspicion, and the two finally came into conflict in 264 BCE.

Tough Lessons

Though new to naval warfare, the Romans managed first to hold and then to turn back the Carthaginian attack. The First Punic War ended with Roman victory in 244 BCE.

The Second Punic War spelled even greater danger. In 218 BCE, the young Carthaginian general Hannibal

▶ Aemilius's decree on the Cádiz tablet held out the promise of freedom for Spain's subjects, though they were now going to live under Roman rule.

20

THE TRANSLATION

WHAT DOES IT MEAN?

Aemilius uses a strategy of divide and rule. He sets out to weaken Hispania's dominant tribes, while winning the support of those who were previously downtrodden.

66 Lucius Aemilius, son of Lucius Imperator, has decreed that the subjects of the Hasta in the Tower of Lascuta shall be set free. Their land and the fort, which they had at the time they should have, and they should keep it as long as the People and Senate of Rome agree. Done in camp on February 12. 99

F·INDERATOR·DECREIVI
IASTENSIVM·SERVEI
SCVTANA·HABITARENT
SENT·AGRVM·oppIDVMqu
TEMPESTATE·posEDISEN
SSIDERE·HABERE·qVE
A·poplVS·SENATVSqVE
ELLEf·ACT·IN·CASTREIS

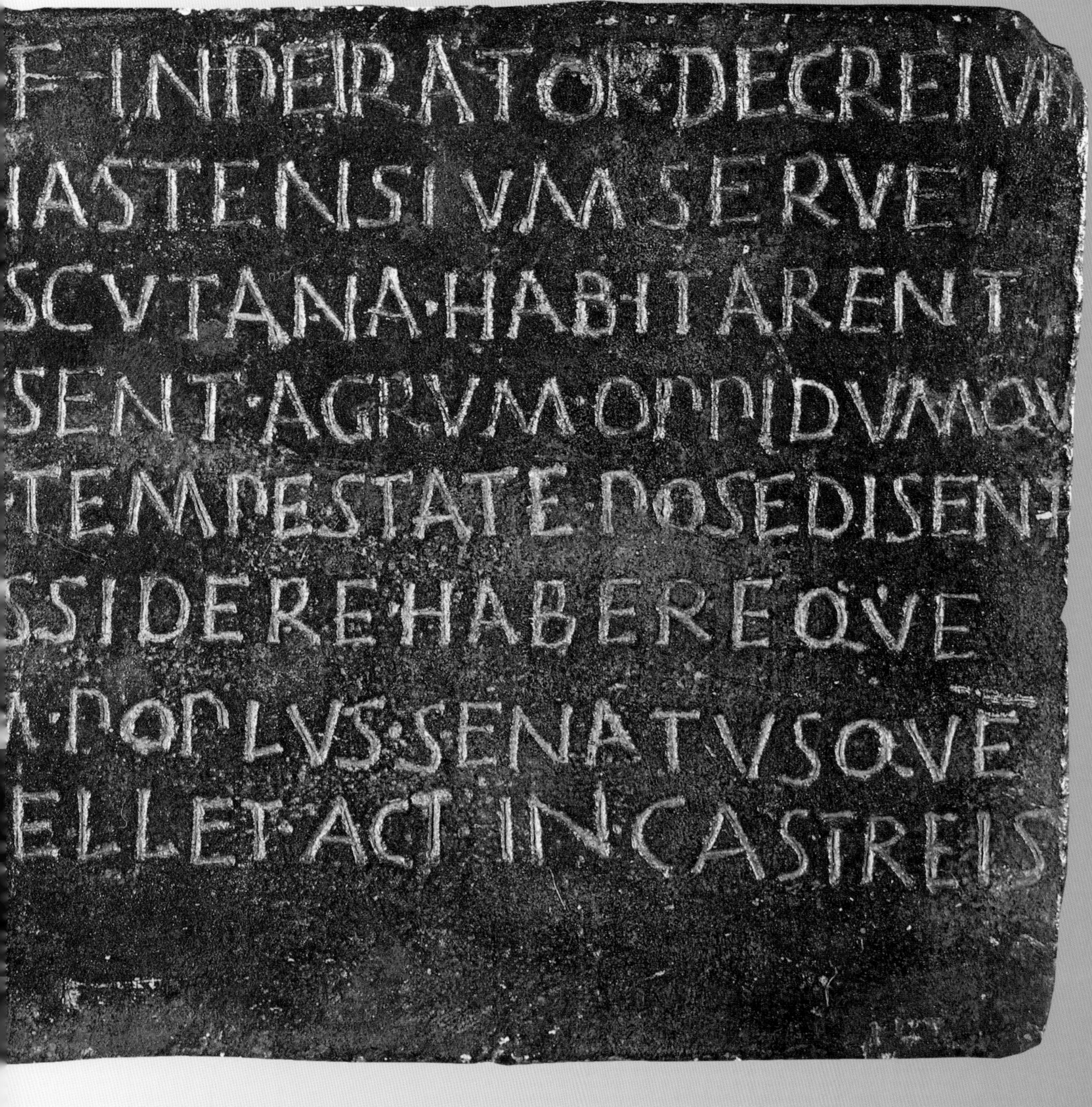

◀ A campaign that promised so much for Hannibal ended in a shattering defeat outside Carthage at the Battle of Zama in 202 BCE.

(248–183 BCE) shipped an army, which included thirty-seven elephants, across the Straits of Gibraltar and into Spain. He then made his way through France and over the Alps (elephants and all) into Italy. His decisive defeat of the Romans at Cannae in 216 BCE brought Rome to the very brink of destruction.

Imperial Arrival

Incredibly, the legions succeeded in clawing their way back to victory when, in 202 BCE, they actually defeated Carthage. Rome had not only survived but had secured an empire. With Carthage gone, the Iberian peninsula stood open, and so Spain and Portugal became the Roman province of Hispania. New territories were also taken in the east, where the Macedonian rulers of Greece and Asia Minor (modern Turkey) had allied themselves with Carthage.

But imperial power brought its own headaches. Even as the last resistance was put down in the east, trouble flared at the far end of the Empire. "All Spain was up in arms," the Roman historian Plutarch (c. 46–120 CE) later reported. But the army sent to sort out the unrest was fortunate in its commander, Lucius Aemilius Paullus (229–160 BCE), Plutarch continued:

> *"Twice he defeated the barbarians in battle; 30,000 of them were killed. These triumphs can be attributed to the resourcefulness of the general in selecting the most advantageous ground and, making his attack at a crucial ford, enabled his men to win an easy victory."*

Tactical Thinking

The Cádiz tablet dates from 189 BCE. It gives us a fascinating insight into Aemilius's way of waging war. He may have been every bit the military genius that Plutarch suggests, but his cunning clearly extended beyond the field of battle into the struggle to win over hearts and minds.

False Freedom?

Those enslaved by the barbarian Hasta tribe were now free, Aemilius announced, and they could have their old lands and stronghold back again.

However, we should not get too carried away in our admiration.

▼ The dry plains and rugged mountains of Iberia were crisscrossed with roads and sprinkled with cities. Hispania became one of the jewels of the Roman Empire.

Like other ancient peoples, the Romans took for granted the right to own people as possessions. Aemilius was more interested in weakening the powerful Hasta tribe by stripping it of its subjects than he was in the rights of their former slaves.

AUGUSTUS'S SHIELD

THE SENATE AWARDED THE *CLUPEUS VIRTUTIS* (SHIELD OF VIRTUE) TO THE FIRST EMPEROR. ON THIS MARBLE PLAQUE WAS INSCRIBED A LIST OF WHAT THE ROMANS SAW AS THE CIVIC VIRTUES.

By the middle of the first century BCE, the Roman Empire was becoming too big to be easily governed. And, more worryingly, so was the Roman army. Charismatic generals inspired such ferocious loyalty in their men that they had enormous military muscle at their command.

The Rise of the Strongman

Julius Caesar (c. 102–44 BCE), the conqueror of Gaul (now France), had been just such a figure. The Senate, alarmed at his mounting influence, recalled him to Rome. He had returned at the head of an invading army, and an adoring public clamored for him to be crowned king. When he made a great show of turning down this honor, their devotion to their hero only grew. However, in 44 BCE, rival patricians assassinated Caesar because they feared they were going to lose all their powers in the Senate to him.

Caesar's friends were outraged at this crime, and at the loss of their own chance of power.

◀ As emperor, Augustus presided over a golden age in art and culture. Here the poet Virgil (70–19 BCE) works on his great Roman epic, the *Aeneid*.

THE TRANSLATION

The inscription on the *clupeus virtutis* shows the importance Romans still attached to their civic duties, even after republican rule had given way to imperial power.

66 The Senate and the Roman people dedicated to the Emperor Augustus, son of Caesar the god, in his Eighth Consulate, the Shield of Virtue, Clemency, Justice, and Piety toward both the gods and the fatherland. 99

▼ The inscription on this marble plaque does remind us that Augustus is the son of Caesar, the god, but it insists that Augustus is emperor because of his own virtues.

SENATVS
POPVLVSQVE ROMANVS
IMP CAESARI DIVI F AVGVSTO
COS VIII DEDIT CLVPEVM
VIRTVTIS CLEMENTIAE
IVSTITIAE PIETATIS ERGA
DEOS PATRIAMQVE

They put pressure on the Senate to proclaim their dead hero a god. A bitter civil war broke out, fought across the entire Roman Empire. Octavian (63 BCE –14 CE), Caesar's adopted son, led the fight against the Senate.

The First Emperor

Finally, in 27 BCE, Octavian defeated his enemies. Thankful to have peace at last, the people hailed him as a hero. But he followed his adoptive father's example in pretending to refuse power. So grateful were the Senate and people for this modesty that (as Octavian must have known they would) they showered him with new honors. As he himself afterward recalled:

"The Senate awarded me the title Augustus [meaning splendid or

▼ The Senate had been the ruling body of the Roman Republic. But, for much of the first century BCE, its power had been trickling away.

august], the doors of my temple were decked with laurel leaves and a civic crown placed above the door to my house, while a golden shield was put up in the Senate House, its inscription bearing witness to my virtue, compassion, justice, and piety—the merits for which the shield had been awarded. From that time on, I was pre-eminent in influence, though in actual power I was not above those fellow-Romans who held magistracy alongside me."

Officially, at least, Augustus was only *primus inter pares* (first among equals). And Augustus was always careful to maintain the illusion that he was just one ruler among several. But as *Princeps* (Principal or First Man), he was unquestionably the man in charge. The days of the Republic were over. Augustus was Rome's first emperor.

Roman Values

As Augustus says, the original *clupeus virtutis* was made of gold. That treasure has long since been lost, but its inscription is clearly preserved in this marble plaque. Did the emperor truly display these qualities? Almost certainly he did not. But that does not mean that the inscription has no interest for us today. How far Augustus actually lived up to the virtues hardly matters. We can still see here the values by which the Romans felt their foremost citizens should live.

▼ Augustus may have been Rome's first emperor, but he followed a long line of military strongmen.

MISSING, PRESUMED DEAD

A TABLET FROM THE RHINELAND COMMEMORATES ONE OF ROME'S RARE MILITARY DEFEATS. THREE WHOLE LEGIONS WERE LOST IN A DISASTROUS ENCOUNTER WITH GERMANIC TRIBESMEN.

This memorial should have marked the grave of a brave and honorable soldier named Marcus Caelius. It was found at Xanten, western Germany, where he had his home. His freedmen, former slaves who felt they owed him their liberty, were buried here, but Marcus Caelius himself was never to have a burial. His mortal remains lay lost on a forest floor.

With him were the bones of thousands of other legionaries, lost in the Varian War of 9 CE. Publius Quinctilius Varus (46 BCE–9 CE), the governor of Roman Germany, launched this doomed venture in response to raids by hostile tribes from the Weser Valley.

A Punitive Action

Varus wanted to teach these unruly natives a lesson, and to do so he brought together an impressive army. It included three legions. One was Marcus Caelius's Eighteenth Legion, and the others were the Seventeenth and Nineteenth. In total, Varus's army numbered some thirty thousand men. All were highly experienced and well trained.

THE TRANSLATION

66 Marcus Caelius's freedmen, Marcus Caelius Privatus, Marcus Caelius Thiaminus. To Marcus Caelius, son of Titus, of the Lemonia voting tribe, from Bononia [probably Bologna], the First Centurion of the Eighteenth Legion. At the age of fifty-three, he fell in the Varian War. The bones of his freedmen are authorized to be buried here. This memorial was raised by his brother Caelius, son of Titus, of the Lemonian tribe. 99

WHAT DOES IT MEAN?

Marcus Caelius's memorial speaks most strongly in its simple dignity. The Roman's patriotic virtue goes without saying. Duty was duty—even at the age of fifty-three.

▶ The Romans had a horror of being left unburied. Marcus Caelius's family made him a particularly fine memorial to compensate for the fact that his body was never found.

M·CAELIVS
M·P·
PRIVATVS

M·CAELIVS
M·L·
THIAMINVS

M·CAELIO·T·F·LEMB·ON
O·LEG·XIIX·ANN·LIII·s
CIDIT·BELLO·VARIANO·OSSA
NFERRE·LICEBIT·P·CAELIVS·T·F
LEM·FRATER·FECIT·

Time and again the Romans had shown that a force like this one had no equal, and a ragtag gathering of tribal fighters could certainly not withstand its might. Such men might be brave and motivated, but they had no answer to the armor, the weaponry, the skills, and, above all, the discipline of a precision-drilled legionary force. A Roman army was an unstoppable machine.

An Army Astray

But this army broke down badly in the boggy ground and dense undergrowth of the Teutoburger Forest. Varus's men had to set aside all their years of drilling and broke from their ranks as they picked their way through tangled thickets and squelched through marshy hollows. They had to keep changing course to avoid tall trees or patches of thorns. The dark wood grew darker as black clouds gathered and rain began to pour.

▼ Even now, and in fine weather, the Teutoburger Forest is eerie. For Rome's lost legions two thousand years ago it must have been a terrifying place.

At some point all military organization was abandoned. Wet through and wretched, the legionaries found their way through the forest as best they could. Many became separated from their comrades. Now disoriented, the entire army drifted without direction.

Varus's Last Stand

Misery turned to terror as showers of spears came down with the driving rain. The Germanic tribesmen appeared out of nowhere between the trees. For three days, they harassed the helpless Romans, picking them off at will. It was a massacre in

▲ *The Nightmare in the Teutoburger Forest*, as imagined by a modern painter. The might of Rome was laid low by Germanic tribesmen.

unbearably slow motion. In the end, indeed, only a few hundred men made it back to base with a horrifying tale of fear and humiliation. Their shame was as great as the grief for Rome.

Varus himself had committed suicide in disgrace, rather than return home to face the consequences, his men reported. When Augustus heard the news he cried, "Quinctilius Varus, give me back my legions!"

◀ Quinctilius Varus's death mask has a gloomy look—as well it might—given his responsibility for the most disastrous defeat ever suffered by a Roman army.

THE GOOD SOLDIER

ROMAN HISTORY INCLUDES GREAT EVENTS AND PERSONALITIES BUT, AS THIS INSCRIPTION FROM RAVENNA REMINDS US, THE EMPIRE WAS BUILT BY THE SELFLESS SERVICE OF ORDINARY MEN.

Who was Marcus Apicius Tirone? His family had his inscription written with pride and, most likely, affection. But what it leaves out is as remarkable as what it includes. For example, it does not say when exactly (or even roughly) this faithful servant of the Empire lived. Scholars believe that his memorial was made around the middle of the first century CE, but even this is just a guess.

A Public Life

What about his personal feelings, or his likes and dislikes? His father is mentioned, but what about his mother?

◀ A Roman—like Augustus here—existed primarily as a public figure. He was a soldier, a statesman, an official of the law, and a priest.

THE TRANSLATION

66 To Marcus Apicius Tirone, son of Tirone of the Camila clan. Primipilus of the Original Twenty-second Legion. Pious and faithful Prefect of the Thirteenth "Twin" Legion. Centurion of Apollo's own Fifteenth Legion. Called to the office of Registrar in the Military Prison with responsibility for wage-lists, he was a city-father for the Municipality of Ravenna and a priest. 99

WHAT DOES IT MEAN?
The words of the inscription of Marcus Apicius emphasize how much a Roman's life was seen to find its fulfillment and its final justification in public service.

▶ Marcus Apicius wanted to be remembered for the work he had done for Ravenna and for Rome. In this inscription, his life is summed up in a simple service record.

Did he have a wife? He was a city-father, we are told, but did he have children? What sort of a relationship did he have with his family? No word of grief is expressed in this inscription.

It does not seem to have occurred to those around him—even to those who must have loved him most—that his more private, human affections could be of any interest.

MAPICIOTF
CAMTIRONI
PPLEG XXII PRIMIG·PF
PRÁEF·LEG·XIII GEM
>LEG XV APOLLINEVOC
ACOMMENT CVST OPTIONI
EVOCSALARCVRATABINDICIB
PATRONMVN RAVEN
PONTIF

his own prestige had to come first. His wife and children would benefit if he was held in high regard, just as they would suffer if he was shamed.

Faithful Service

This family had every reason to be proud of Marcus Apicius. He had served in no fewer than three legions. The Thirteenth became the "twin" in

What mattered to them, and what made him the man he was, and what his caring family was most concerned to list, were his services to the Roman Empire and to the city of Ravenna. We should not be too surprised by this. We know now from a number of written sources that the Romans placed a much greater value on public life than we do now.

The main concern for the Roman citizen was to secure what was known as *existimatio* (public reputation or civic honor), and it is the origin of our modern word "esteem." But it also comes from the same root as the verb *existere* (to stand out from).

The Romans did not make the sort of distinction we do between the private individual and the public figure; without his public reputation the Roman did not exist. However much the Roman citizen loved his family,

▶ Caesar's Thirteenth Legion crosses the Rubicon River in 49 BCE. Rome had always been a military power and, increasingly, the legions were making Roman history.

34

31 BCE. Badly savaged in the civil war, it had to be replenished with men from other legions, and was known as *gemina* (twin) from that time on. As *Primipilus* (first javelin) for the Twenty-second Legion, Marcus Apicius was the centurion of the legion's so-called First Century, the unit that led the others into battle. The Fifteenth Legion was stationed in Pannonia (modern-day Hungary) in Marcus Apicius's time. This would have been a tough posting in itself, but the legion was also sent east to put down rebellions in Armenia, Judea (Israel), and Parthia (Iran).

His days of fighting over, Marcus Apicius moved into military administration and, from there, into the government and religious administration of Ravenna.

ASELLINA'S DINER

OUTSIDE A *CAUPONA* (FOOD STAND) IN POMPEII IS THIS BRIEF, HANDWRITTEN MENU, DECORATED TO ATTRACT PASSERSBY.

Mount Vesuvius is a volcano. Though quiet for a long time now, it still looms menacingly above the Bay of Naples in southern Italy. One day in 79 CE, it erupted without warning, spouting sparks and flames into the sky. Quickly, though, clouds of gray-white ash blotted out these fireworks.

▼ Lollius was very lucky to have the political weight of the girls at Asellina's behind him. Who knows? Their influence may well have won him some votes among the regulars at the food stand.

Hurled high by the blast, the ash drifted down over a wide area. A deadly snow, it blanketed the earth beneath. The cities of Pompeii and Herculaneum were engulfed, suffocating the inhabitants as they went about their everyday business.

Fast Food

Excavations have been going on at Pompeii since the eighteenth century. The discoveries have not just been historically fascinating but also full of human interest.

THE TRANSLATION

66 Shoppers, in the kitchen we have chicken, fish, pork, peacock 99

WHAT DOES IT MEAN?

Asellina's straightforward menu would have inspired confidence, and the decorative touches that have been added (a heart, a spoked wheel, and a squiggly plant or herb) add an air of friendliness.

▲ Asellina's menu is attractive and neatly done. Care has obviously been taken to get it just right. However, there is a homespun feeling to it, which gives it a special charm.

37

Over time, archaeologists have uncovered a community frozen to the spot. Many marvelous artistic treasures have been found, yet humbler, everyday finds have often seemed to touch us more.

Asellina's *caupona* is a good example. This was an ancient food stand or diner. There was space inside for people who wanted to take a bit more time over their meal, but anyone in a hurry could just buy what they wanted at a counter that opened onto the street.

Ordinary Romans relied on what we would call fast food because few had facilities to cook at home. Most people lived in overcrowded timber-built apartment buildings called *insulae* (islands). It would have been very dangerous to try to light a stove inside one of these buildings.

A snack of goat's cheese, olives, and herbs was one thing, but cooking hot food was impossible. So, for a hot meal you would go to a *caupona* or a food stand of some sort on the street.

A Stake in the Community

There was nothing stylish about a place like Asellina's, and it is not clear what choice (if any) you had as to how the chicken, fish, pork, or peacock were prepared. But what the customer would have wanted in a place like this was good, home cooking and friendly

◄ This wall painting from a Pompeii bakery shows the owner handing out loaves. Often the most ordinary finds turn out to be something we can all identify with, which makes them all the more interesting.

▲ One of the big surprises of the Pompeii excavations has been the amount of electoral graffiti found. Clearly this is evidence that the city's political life was lively and exciting.

service. Asellina's menu has a handcrafted look, which would have helped make diners feel at home.

Then as now, catering work was poorly paid. The staff in a *caupona* would have been women. Not only that, but they would probably have been foreigners who did not have the rights even of Roman women. In spite of this, it seems that over time they came to feel a sort of friendship for their regular customers and a sense of belonging in the community in which they worked.

So, even though they were just about the last people ever to have been consulted over the government of Pompeii, they took a lively interest in its politics. We know this because another hastily painted inscription at Asellina's, on the other side of the door from the menu, makes that clear:

66 The girls at Asellina's—especially Zmyrina—ask you to vote for C. Lollius Fuscus as duumvir for roads and for sacred and public buildings. 99

A duumvir was one of two men in charge of important projects in the city. Zmyrina and her colleagues clearly felt it mattered who was elected to these posts.

MR. POMPEII

MARCUS HOLCONIUS RUFUS SET HIS STAMP ON THE CITY OF POMPEII, JUST AS HE HAD HIS NAME AND RESUMÉ CARVED INTO THE STEPS OF ITS GREAT THEATER.

We do not know his birth- or death-dates, but for several decades toward the end of the first century CE, Marcus Holconius Rufus was Mr. Pompeii. An entrepreneur, he owned a brickworks there, but he also earned money running an important wine business. Thanks to the success of those ventures he became a very wealthy man.

▼ A Roman wine store imagined by a modern painter. Wine was an important commodity in the Roman world and it provided the basis for Marcus Holconius Rufus's fortune.

Buying Prestige

He was an extremely influential man. The Romans loved luxury as much as anyone else but, as far as they were concerned, it was not the most important thing money could buy. The main reason for getting rich, the Romans felt, was the *fama* (fame) and *existimatio* (public reputation or civic honor) they could gain by pouring money into public projects. So, once he had made his fortune, Marcus Holconius Rufus set about spending it on the sort of things that would bring him civic honor.

The two most important officials in any Roman city were its two duumvir. Together, they acted as judges in court cases and saw to the collection of taxes in the city. But no one was taxed more heavily than they were themselves.

THE TRANSLATION

66 To Marcus Holconius, son of Marcus Rufus, five times Duumvir (of which two Quinquennial), voted Military Tribune by the people, Flamen of Augustus, Patron of the Colony. By the decree of the Decurions. 99

WHAT DOES IT MEAN?

The crucial thing about this inscription is where it is placed. It is found beside the seat belonging to Marcus Holconius Rufus in the very theater he had built. Its presence seals the bond between Marcus Holconius Rufus and Pompeii for all time.

▲ This inscription, carved into the stone of the step, marked Marcus Holconius Rufus's *bisellium* (double seat), much like the dignitaries' box in a theater today.

No candidate could hope to secure the votes he needed to become a duumvir unless he was seen as a generous benefactor, funding the gladiator contests, sports events, stage plays, music festivals, and all the other spectacles the people loved. He might even have to put up money for major public building projects. And that was how Marcus Holconius Rufus came to fund this theater.

Imperial Priest

He obviously won the support he needed because he was elected duumvir not once but five times, and two of those terms lasted for five years, rather than the customary one. Being elected military tribune was actually no great achievement, and was probably among his earliest public posts.

▼ Based on Greek models, the Roman theater was an open-air structure. The seating was divided, with important officials and leading citizens positioned at the front.

▶ In his day, Marcus Holconius Rufus was the leading citizen of Pompeii. He was a businessman, a benefactor, a politician, and a priest.

But his election to the office of flamen is more striking. The flamen was a sort of priest, officially appointed by the state to supervise the cult of a particular god or goddess on its behalf.

Although it was a distinguished position, it was not out of the ordinary, except that Marcus Holconius Rufus was to serve the god Augustus. Having had his adoptive father, Julius Caesar (c. 102–44 BCE), proclaimed a god, Augustus (63 BCE–14 CE) had now bestowed the same honor upon himself.

Later emperors did the same and in time it would be taken for granted. For the moment, though, the idea was new and still a little strange. In fact, Marcus Holconius Rufus is the first flamen of this sort that we know of anywhere in Italy.

Hard Feelings

His position as Patron of the Colony, meanwhile, made him a sort of Pompeiian ambassador to Rome. This was an important and challenging role because there were constant tensions between the outlying parts of the Empire and its center.

Rome was widely seen (and resented) as unfairly living off of what the provinces worked hard to produce.

Many people in the wider Empire also felt that Roman officials knew nothing of life beyond their immediate surroundings in Rome.

43

A MUSICIAN'S MEMORIAL

HERE LIES LUTATIA, A TEENAGE MUSICIAN. HER MONUMENT MAKES IT CLEAR HOW MUCH SHE WAS MISSED AND HOW LIMITED THE FUNDS WERE FOR HER COMMEMORATION.

◄ Mosaics surviving from Roman times have revealed a wide range of musical instruments. At first glance they may seem exotic, but their resemblance to modern instruments is clear.

The most celebrated ancient monuments are timeless works of truly incredible artistry. No expense was spared when it came to commemorating emperors, generals, and other dignitaries. The finest stone was used and the most skillful sculptors were employed.

But what sort of monuments could ordinary people expect? Many, perhaps most, must have had unmarked graves. But every Roman must have longed for a memorial of some sort. Lutatia Lupata's

THE TRANSLATION

66 In the name of the gods and the ancestral spirits. Lutatia Lupata, aged sixteen. Lutatia Severa set this up in memory of her foster daughter.
Here she lies.
May the earth rest lightly upon you. 99

WHAT DOES IT MEAN?

Lutatia Lutapa's stela tells us that ordinary Romans wanted to be remembered as much as their rulers did, and that finer feelings were not exclusive to the patrician class.

▶ Awkward it may be, but Lutatia Severa's memorial for her student and adopted daughter still speaks to us of the love she must have felt.

D   M   S
LVTATIA LVPATA ANN XVI
LVTATIA SEVERA ALVMN
H S E S T T L

DID YOU KNOW?

The supposedly Spanish guitar was not brought to Iberia (Portugal and Spain) until the Moorish conquest of the eighth century CE. Both the Greeks and the Romans had adopted the Persian *kithara*, but this was more like a harp, without a neck. The Roman *pandurium* was an early form of the mandolin, though it usually had only three strings. All we can say is that there seem to have been a number of different stringed instruments of this type and that Lutatia probably performed on one of these.

monument was discovered in 1956 by archaeologists investigating a Roman necropolis outside Mérida in southwestern Spain. At some point, the stela had fallen forward and was lying face down in the dirt. It may have been an undignified position, but the dirt protected the stela from damage through the centuries.

A Labor of Love

Some might feel that it was hardly worth saving because there are any number of more accomplished ancient sculptures. In fact, whoever made Lutatia Lupata's stele was not very skilled. The inscription is clumsily done because the letters are cramped and crooked and their spacing is erratic. The lines slant slightly to the right. As for the figure, its oversized head seems to be bursting out of a framing arch that has been made too small. The strumming fingers look like something a child in kindergarten made with clay.

◄ Music was ever-present in Roman life. Groups of players performed in the streets or were hired to entertain guests at feasts and banquets.

Lutatia Severa, who set up the stela, clearly asked the craftsman to take on more than he could handle. This is a monument that was made with bargain-basement skills.

And yet, with all these weaknesses, the memorial is truly touching. In fact, it is much more moving than many artistically finer works because its awkward lack of grace only seems to make the message more sincere.

An Unusual Relationship

Like young ladies of other ages, Roman girls from patrician families learned to play musical instruments. But Lutatia Lupata's memorial would shame a family of the ruling class. It is much more likely that both Lutatia Lupata and her stepmother Lutatia Severa were professional musicians. Being a musician in the Roman Empire did not bring much prestige and those in the trade were not

▲ Mérida was one of the great cities of the Roman world. This stunning theater is just one of its many marvelous monuments from that time.

paid well. This is probably the reason for the inferior quality of this monument. Yet Lutatia Lupata clearly still took enough pride in her musical skills for her stepmother to want them recorded for posterity in her memorial. So she has been portrayed in her monument strumming away for eternity.

Lutatia Severa's relationship with Lutatia Lupata must have been a complicated one. The dead girl was apparently a freed slave who she had adopted as her foster daughter. But she was also her alumna (student). In fact, she was probably her apprentice, and was being trained as an assistant. Whatever sort of professional relationship they may have had as musicians, the bond of love between them is evident twenty centuries on.

A GRAVESTONE FOR A GLADIATOR

A WIDOW HAD THIS STELA SET UP AS A SIMPLE MEMORIAL TO HER GLADIATOR HUSBAND. HE MAY HAVE BEEN A PROFESSIONAL KILLER, YET HE WAS ALSO A BELOVED FAMILY MAN.

Akhisar, in Turkey, was for centuries the Greek colony of Thyatira. By the second century CE, the Greek world had long been in Roman hands, but Thyatira still thrived as a center for the dyeing trade. This was a very ordinary city, then, and Ammias's Greek inscription commemorated an ordinary man.

▼ It was one of history's greatest civilizations, yet the Roman Empire had a brutal side. Men and animals were made to fight to the death for the entertainment of an audience.

Though the sculpted relief makes Araxios's profession clear, we have no way of knowing if his career killed him. Did he die in the arena, or was he taken by old age?

Respectable Killers?

Gladiators were not supposed to be ordinary—modern moviemakers and the ancient chroniclers both agree on this. The men, who swaggered out into the arena to fight and to triumph or to die before baying crowds, were the most murderous, the most desperate of desperadoes, and the scum of the earth. For the most part they were condemned criminals, who chose the chance of life in the arena over the certainty of execution. They lived on the edge—one moment victorious, the next perhaps savagely slaughtered.

THE TRANSLATION

WHAT DOES IT MEAN?

Araxios's memorial is a reminder of just how far even a Greek-speaking city of Asia Minor had embraced Roman culture by the second century CE.

66 Ammias, for Araxios, also known as Antaios, of Daldis. To her husband in memory. **99**

▼ Araxios's curved *sica* sits oddly with his heavy un-Thracian armor, scholars say. But there is no arguing with the moving simplicity of his wife's inscription.

▲ Antaios and Hercules are joined in a life-and-death struggle. Gaia's son loses his advantage as the Greek hero hoists him high above the earth.

The Romans despised them yet romanticized them at the same time.

Here, however, we have an apparently respectable member of society, mourned at very least by his wife, and perhaps by a family. Strange as it seems, there is in fact evidence that, whatever happened in Rome itself, in the further reaches of the Roman Empire things were often very different. With the legions crying out for men, even hardened criminals could not be spared so novel ways of raising gladiators were found.

Researchers at Augusta Rarica, outside Basel in Switzerland, suggest that many worked part-time, following other occupations between the great festivals (if they survived).

A Thracian With a Difference

Araxios is also different in the way he is armed. Strict rules supposedly governed gladiators' weaponry and armor. In the early Republic, historians believe, when prisoners of war were forced to fight for their lives in the gladiators' arena they would have used the traditional weaponry and armor of their nations.

Araxios's stela shows him holding a short, curved *sica* (dagger-sword), which was the trademark weapon of the Thracian gladiator. But in other ways, he does not look like a Thracian. Heavily armored, he peers over the top of a large rectangular shield. Thracian gladiators, in contrast, were lightly armed and mobile. They carried a *parma* (a small round shield), wore protective leg-greaves, and carried a *sica*.

What are we to make of these oddities? Was it that, this far from Rome, the rules of the arena were a little more relaxed or was it just that the sculptor got the style of the armor wrong?

▲ The curved helmets of the gladiator helped to deflect all but the hardest, most direct of blows. Most versions had some sort of visor for the face.

THE CHRISTIANS ARE COMING!

EARLY IN THE FOURTH CENTURY CE, THE GOOD PAGAN PEOPLE OF ARYCANDA IN TURKEY SENT OUT A PLEA FOR PROTECTION FROM THOSE SHAMELESS, GODLESS MISBELIEVERS, THE CHRISTIANS.

By the end of the third century, the Roman Empire was a very different place. For a start, it had not one emperor but four. The Empire was so big and sprawling, with so many threats on so many borders, that it was more than one ruler could realistically handle.

▼ Few Christians were actually thrown to the lions, but many lost their lives in the waves of bloody persecution that arose occasionally between the long periods of time when the Christians *were* tolerated.

In 285 CE, Diocletian (reigned from 284 to 305 CE) appointed Maximian (reigned from 286 to 305 CE) his Augustus in the West, or coruler. Later, in 293 CE, he inaugurated the tetrarchy (rule of four), creating two assistant emperors to share the burden. Constantius (reigned from 305 to 306 CE) ruled in the West and Galerius (reigned from 305 to 311 CE), ruled in the East.

THE TRANSLATION

66 To the saviors of all humanity, the divine Augustuses ... The gods of your fathers having shown, O glorious rulers, that they look after those who see to the defense of religion, we believe that, for the sake of your eternal fortune, supreme lords and masters, that, calling upon your immortal and imperial power, you should insist that the Christians, so long rebellious even into our own time, should be destroyed and forced to renounce their crazy notions of removing the honors to which the true gods are entitled. Though of the greatest benefit to your loyal subjects, this can only be achieved if you step in and use your immortal and divine authority to put a stop to these wicked atheists, enemies of true religion and insist that, for the remainder of your incorruptible reigns, they practice the rites due to the ancestral gods. 99

▶ It is strange today to see Christians being denounced for their godless atheism, but that is how it must have seemed to those who believed in the old ways.

A Convenient Scapegoat

These adjustments seem trivial beside the great development of those times, which was the rising influence of Christianity. But this was still very much a minority religion and that minority was sometimes persecuted. Notoriously, the emperor Nero (reigned from 54 to 68 CE) blamed the Christians for the great fire of Rome

▼ The great fire of Rome in 64 CE burned for six days and seven nights, according to the historian Suetonius, damaging large parts of Rome. Many Romans lived in wooden houses.

in 64 CE, and made them a scapegoat. Like many minorities, the Christians were attacked in times of economic crisis, but there were lengthy periods when they were tolerated.

Diocletian was tolerant by nature, but the same pressures that drove him to divide his empire made him turn on the Christians. In 303 CE he called for churches to be demolished and Christians enslaved. Claims that ten thousand were martyred in a single day are probably exaggerated, but it seems certain that many thousands were murdered.

An Affront to the Old Ways

Anti-Christian feeling was not just something that flared up from time to time. People saw Christianity as threatening all that they held sacred. Some, perhaps, were motivated by a more generalized fear of change. They felt more comfortable keeping faith with what they knew.

Growing confusion at the top only heightened their nervousness because the four emperors were pulling in different ways. Constantius had never felt happy with the persecution of the Christians. And even in the East, Galerius was reviewing his position. He had been ferocious in his onslaught against the

Christians, but by 310 CE he was coming to the conclusion that they might be more easily managed if they were no longer the outcasts of society. In 311 CE, ironically, even as the people of Arycanda were calling for a crackdown, he was issuing a new edict of toleration.

▶ Constantine I made Christianity the official religion of the Roman Empire, bringing centuries of random outbreaks of persecution to an end once and for all.

HAIRAN'S TOMB

HERE IS A MAJESTIC TOMB WITH A GRAND TRILINGUAL INSCRIPTION.
BUT HAIRAN'S MONUMENT WOULD HAVE BEEN EVEN MORE
IMPRESSIVE IF HIS LATIN HAD NOT BEEN FULL OF MISTAKES.

Syria had belonged to the Roman Empire since 64 BCE, but the eastern city of Palmyra had not become a part. It was not until the first century CE that Palmyra was conquered, and even then it had remained un-Romanized.

The Roman Way

The Romans always claimed to have brought civilization to barbarous countries. No doubt they truly thought this was the case. But the tribal peoples they conquered were not the savages the Romans would have us believe, even if we are only now beginning to appreciate how sophisticated their societies and cultures were.

However, in many newly conquered countries, the Roman way seemed obviously preferable to the barbarism of life before the Romans arrived. At the very least there was something undeniably impressive about Roman roads and buildings and Roman laws and systems of government. The luxurious Roman customs of banquets and bathing also had a glamorous appeal.

▼ The Latin text comes first in Hairan's inscription, though, as the mistakes make clear, it trailed a distant third in the list of his languages.

immortal—Living forever; a deity or spirit, rather than a living man or woman.

legion—The basic unit into which the Roman army was divided. Each legion might have anything between three thousand and six thousand men, including both infantry and cavalry. Each legion amounted to a small army in itself.

maritime—Having to do with the sea or seafaring.

mortal—Liable to die, so used to describe any ordinary man or woman, as opposed to a god or goddess or spirit, who is immortal and so lives forever.

mosaic—A pattern or picture made up from lots of small fragments of colored glass or broken tiles.

necropolis—A large cemetery or, literally, a city of the dead, it comes from the Greek words *nekro* (dead) and *polis* (city).

patricians—Members of the leading families of Rome.

peninsula—Literally, in Latin, an almost-island: an area of land surrounded on three sides by sea.

Punic—Inhabitants of Carthage, from the Latin *punicus.*

republic—A state in which power belongs to the people, rather than a king or other ruler.

sack—To plunder and destroy a settlement, temple, or city.

shrine—Any place or building that is holy.

stela—A standing stone monument, inscribed with words or pictures (or both).

subject—Someone who is under the authority or the dominance of another.

tyrannize—A tyrant is an all-powerful ruler who governs on the basis of his or her own personal whim. To tyrannize is to rule in this way.

usurp—To take a position that belongs by rights to someone else. A "usurper" might bring down a king and take his throne for himself or herself.

TIMELINE OF ROME

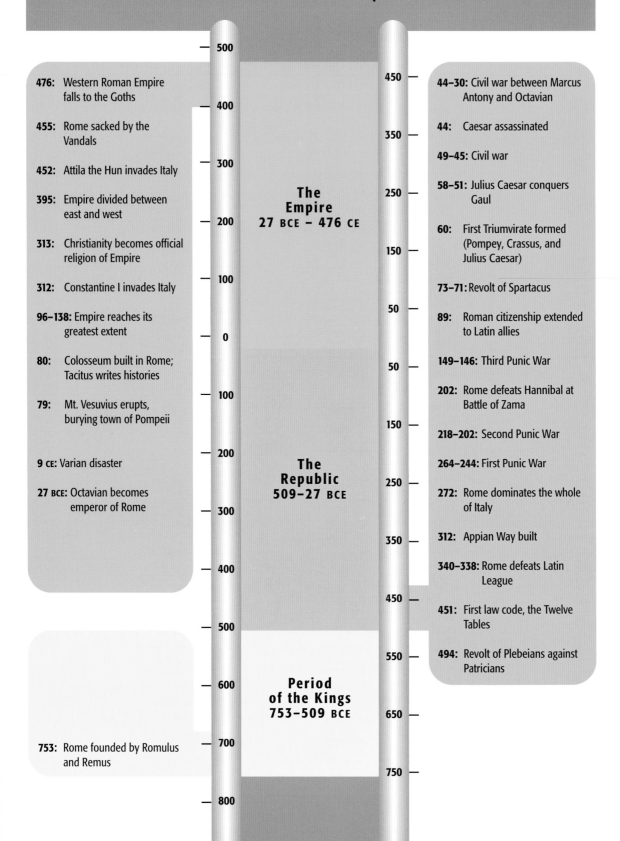

The Empire
27 BCE – 476 CE

The Republic
509–27 BCE

Period of the Kings
753–509 BCE

476: Western Roman Empire falls to the Goths

455: Rome sacked by the Vandals

452: Attila the Hun invades Italy

395: Empire divided between east and west

313: Christianity becomes official religion of Empire

312: Constantine I invades Italy

96–138: Empire reaches its greatest extent

80: Colosseum built in Rome; Tacitus writes histories

79: Mt. Vesuvius erupts, burying town of Pompeii

9 CE: Varian disaster

27 BCE: Octavian becomes emperor of Rome

753: Rome founded by Romulus and Remus

44–30: Civil war between Marcus Antony and Octavian

44: Caesar assassinated

49–45: Civil war

58–51: Julius Caesar conquers Gaul

60: First Triumvirate formed (Pompey, Crassus, and Julius Caesar)

73–71: Revolt of Spartacus

89: Roman citizenship extended to Latin allies

149–146: Third Punic War

202: Rome defeats Hannibal at Battle of Zama

218–202: Second Punic War

264–244: First Punic War

272: Rome dominates the whole of Italy

312: Appian Way built

340–338: Rome defeats Latin League

451: First law code, the Twelve Tables

494: Revolt of Plebeians against Patricians

FURTHER INFORMATION

BOOKS

Hinds, Kathryn. *Everyday Life in the Roman Empire*. New York: Marshall Cavendish, 2010.

Reece, Katherine. *The Romans: Builders of an Empire* (Ancient Civilizations). Vero Beach, FL: Rourke Publishing, 2006.

Schomp, Virginia. *The Ancient Romans* (Myths of the World). New York: Marshall Cavendish, 2009.

Scurman, Ike, and John Malam. *Ancient Roman Civilization* (Ancient Civilizations and Their Myths and Legends). New York: Rosen Publishing, 2009.

WEBSITES

The British Museum: Ancient Rome —www.britishmuseum.org/explore/world_cultures/europe/ancient_rome.aspx

History for Kids: Ancient Rome—www.historyforkids.org/learn/romans

Odyssey Online: Rome—www.carlos.emory.edu/ODYSSEY/ROME/homepg.html

PBS: Rome in the First Century C.E.—www.pbs.org/empires/romans

THE AUTHOR

Michael Kerrigan has written dozens of books for children and young adults over the last twenty years. He is the author of *The Ancients in Their Own Words* (2008), *A Dark History: The Roman Emperors* (2008), and *Ancient Greece and the Mediterranean* (part of the BBC Ancient Civilizations series). He also works as a columnist, book reviewer, and feature writer for publications including the *Scotsman* and the *Times Literary Supplement*. He lives in Edinburgh, Scotland.

INDEX